ISBN: 9798379212858

Imprint: Independently published

Contents Page

Introduction

Welcome to the Tottenham Hotspur Biographies for Kids. I hope you're raring to learn about 25 legends of this amazing football club! (All of the players included are former players and not current players).

Each player's biography will start with a full-size image so that you are able to recognise them in future if you don't already! This will be followed by two pages of information starting with a few stats which are date of birth, year of Spurs debut, nationality, position, height and major trophies won during their time at the club (including Charity Shields and Super Cups).

Next, you'll get an overview of their early career, late career, accomplishments and a summary with a particular focus on their Spurs careers. Enjoy!

White Hart Lane in October 1965 in a game against West Bromwich Albion. This picture is looking towards the West Stand and Paxton Road End.

Trophy Cabinet

First Division (2)
1950–51, 1960–61

Second Division (2)
1919–20, 1949–50

FA Cup (8)
1900–01, 1920–21, 1960–61, 1961–62, 1966–67, 1980–81, 1981–82, 1990–91

League Cup (4)
1970–71, 1972–73, 1998–99, 2007–08

Charity Shield (7)
1921, 1951, 1961, 1962, 1967*, 1981*, 1991* (*shared)

UEFA Cup (2)
1971–72, 1983–84

UEFA Cup Winners' Cup (1)
1962–63

OSSIE ARDILES

Born: 3rd of August 1952
Debut: 1978
Nationality: Argentinian
Position: Midfielder
Height: 5 ft 7 in (1.70 m)
Major Trophies: 4

Early Career

Born in the city of Cordoba in Argentina, Osvaldo Cesar Ardiles played football in the streets and was given the nickname 'Pitón' (python) by his brother because of his snake-like dribbling skills. He studied for a law degree but gave that up after deciding to pursue a career in professional football. He made his first team debut in 1973 for Instituto de Córdoba, before a short spell at Belgrano. He then joined Huracán in 1975 where he made 113 league appearances in four years. Having made his international debut for Argentina in 1975, Ardiles was selected for the World Cup finals in his home country in 1978. He competed in six games including the final as Argentina won the tournament for the first time.

Later Career

After the World Cup, Ardiles and his Argentine teammate Ricardo 'Ricky' Villa made a surprise move to Spurs and made his debut against Nottingham Forest a month later. He was a regular starter and scored a wonder goal at Old Trafford to knock United out of the 1979/80 FA Cup. He scored a personal-best five league goals for the club during the 1980/81 season helping Spurs to win the 1981 FA Cup Final after a replay against Manchester City. To commemorate the victory, Ardiles and the rest of the Spurs squad collaborated with pop duo Chas & Dave for a song, "Ossie's Dream" which reached number five in the charts. After coming runners-up in the League Cup, and reaching the semi-finals of the Cup Winners' Cup in 1982, Ardiles was a major factor in Spurs reaching the FA Cup Final for the second successive season. He played a big part in the semi-final win over Leicester City. However, he was unable to play in the final as he had to join up with the Argentina squad in preparation for the 1982 World Cup hosted in Spain. At that World Cup, he strangely wore the number 1 shirt as Argentina gave out numbers in alphabetical order at the time. Due to the breakout of the Falklands War between the UK and his home nation, Ardiles decided not to go back to Spurs for a season, and instead joined French side Paris Saint-Germain on loan. After a short while, he joined up with Tottenham again in January 1983. He suffered from a long series of injuries but managed to help the team triumph in the UEFA Cup in 1984, coming on as a substitute in the second leg of the final. After the FA Cup Final in 1987, Ardiles became the caretaker coach in the autumn, before leaving the club in 1988. He played for a few clubs before returning to Spurs to become their manager in 1993 and in doing so, became the Premier League's first ever Argentine manager. He went on to coach over a dozen teams over a 20-year period all around the world.

Accomplishments

Ardiles played 417 games for Spurs and netted 37 goals. He won the FA Cup twice, and the UEFA Cup once with the club. He won 51 caps for Argentina and scored eight goals, winning the World Cup on home soil in 1978. He was a Tottenham Hotspur Hall of Fame inductee in 2008.

Summary: Described as one of football's first cult heroes, Ardiles along with Villa are footballing pioneers after becoming the first overseas players to play in England's First Division. His small frame meant he excelled technically, particularly at dribbling and close control.

GARETH BALE

Born: 16th of July 1989
Debut: 2007
Nationality: Welsh
Position: Winger
Height: 6 ft 1 in (1.85 m)
Major Trophies: 0

Early Career

Born in the capital of Wales, Cardiff, Gareth Frank Bale was first noticed by English side Southampton at the age of nine, and he soon joined their youth ranks. In April 2006, he became the second-youngest player to represent the Saints at just 16 years of age. Nearly four months later, he scored his first goal for the club from a free-kick. Bale made his debut for the Wales national team in the same year and became the youngest to play for them at the time. He signed for Spurs in May 2007 at the age of 17 for an initial £5m and played his first game under two months later.

Later Career

His first goal for the club came against Fulham before scoring the winning goal against arch-rivals Arsenal with a free kick. After being named Welsh Player of the Year in 2010, Bale was propelled onto the world stage with a stunning hat-trick against the reigning European Champions Inter Milan at the San Siro. The team narrowly lost 4-3 after being 4-0 down, but Bale tormented the Inter defence, setting up two of the goals in the second leg in a Man of the Match performance to help Spurs reach the next round. He recorded his first Premier League hat-trick on Boxing Day in 2012 against Aston Villa and netted with two trademark free kicks in a Europa League game later in the season. He scored 21 league goals in the 2012/13 season and was named

PFA Player of the Year and Young Player of the Year. Bale then made a world record £85.3m move to Spanish giants Real Madrid. He scored on his La Liga debut and his goal against rivals Barcelona in the dying stages of the 2014 Copa del Rey Final was considered one of the great goals in the competition's history. He scored a goal in extra-time against Atlético Madrid to secure Real their tenth Champions League title after a 12-year wait. In the 2018 Champions League Final, Bale became the first substitute to score twice in a Champions League final and was named Man of the Match, the first goal, considered one of the greatest Champions League goals in history was an overhead kick from 18-yards. He later went on to become the highest-scoring British player in the Spanish league. He went back to Tottenham Hotspur in 2020 on loan and scored 11 goals in 20 league games during the season.

Accomplishments

Bale played 237 games for Spurs scoring 71 goals across two spells. With Real Madrid, he scored 106 goals in 258 games. His honours include three La Liga titles, and a staggering five Champions League triumphs with Real. With the Welsh national team, he has won over 100 caps and scored a record 38 goals so far. He has been named Welsh footballer of the year six times and has led Wales to two European Championship campaigns and their first World Cup since 1958 in 2022. Bale is the first Welshman to score a goal in a European Cup/Champions League Final.

Summary: Gareth Bale has been considered one of the greatest wingers of his generation. He is known for his pace, long-range shooting and as a free-kick specialist. He is widely regarded as the greatest ever Welsh player and has won a joint-second highest number of Champions League titles with five.

DANNY BLANCHFLOWER

Born: 10th of February 1926
Debut: 1954
Nationality: Northern Irish
Position: Midfielder
Height: 5 ft 9 in (1.75 m)
Makor Trophies: 4

Early career

Robert Dennis Blanchflower was born in the capital city of Northern Ireland, Belfast. His mother was a football player. He was awarded a scholarship to attend the Belfast College of Technology. He left early though and joined the Royal Air Force in 1943. In 1946, at the age of 20, he was back in Belfast, and he signed for Glentoran. He played in the senior side for three years before signing for Barnsley in 1949 for £6,000 at the age of 23 before signing for Aston Villa for £15,000 two years later.

Later Career

He appeared in over 150 games for the club, before again moving, this time to First Division Tottenham Hotspur in 1954 for £30,000. He played his first game a few days later, and then became the team captain the following year, before skippering the Northern Ireland team to the quarter-final of the World Cup in 1958. He was the team captain as Spurs won the first 11 league games at the start of the 1960/61 season, a record for the top division of English football, eventually finishing eight points clear of second place. By beating Leicester City in the FA Cup Final, Spurs became the first team in the 20th century to complete the League and Cup double in English domestic football and the first in 64 years. Blanchflower was voted the Football Writers' Association Footballer of the Year in 1961 having previously received the accolade in 1958. He converted a penalty in the 1962 FA Cup Final against Burnley as Spurs made it back-to-back wins in the competition. A year later, he was the skipper again, as he led the side to a European Cup Winners' Cup success over defending champions Atlético Madrid. Whilst with Tottenham, he also made a few appearances for Canadian side Toronto City in 1961, playing alongside Stanley Matthews and Johnny Haynes. He eventually retired as a player in April 1964 at the age of 38. He had captained the side to four major trophies during his time with the club. The last game of his career came in South Africa in 1965. Blanchflower coached at Spurs for a few years, and then became manager of Northern Ireland and Chelsea. He also did some television work during and after his career. In May 1990, he was honoured with a testimonial match.

Accomplishments

Blanchflower made 337 league appearances in ten years at Spurs, and played 382 matches in total, scoring 21 goals. He won the league title once, the FA Cup twice, and the Cup Winners' Cup once. For Northern Ireland, he earned 56 caps and scored two goals. He was the first player to attain 50 caps for his country and was named in the 1958 FIFA World Cup All-Star Team. He was inducted into the English Football Hall of Fame in 2003.

Summary: Danny Blanchflower was a club legend, known for his passing skills and inspirational leadership qualities. He captained Spurs to their first and only double. He was ranked as the greatest player ever in Spurs history by The Times newspaper in 2009. He passed away in December 1993.

MARTIN CHIVERS

Born: 27th of April 1945
Debut: 1968
Nationality: English
Position: Forward
Height: 6 ft 1 in (1.85 m)
Major Trophies: 3

Early Career

Born in the port city of Southampton, Martin Harcourt Chivers sent a letter to Southampton asking for a trial whilst still at school. He was invited to play in the nursery side before being given the chance to become a professional in September 1962. He made his first team debut a few days later, aged 17, and netted his first goal in April in his third outing. The following season, Chivers was joint top goalscorer for the club with 21 goals, competing in the Second Division. He was instrumental in seeing the side gain promotion during the 1965/66 season with a career-best 30 goals in 39 matches, with all the goals coming from his first 29 games.

Later Career

After scoring over 100 goals for the club, Chivers decided to move on and signed for fellow First Division team Tottenham Hotspur in early 1968 for a British record fee of £125,000. He struck on his debut a few days later, and his first hat-trick came early in the 1968/69 season. In the 1970/71 season, he helped Spurs to finish third in the league with 34 goals in 58 games, 21 of them in the league and scored both goals as Spurs beat Aston Villa in the League Cup Final. He scored a personal best 44 goals the following season in 64 appearances. He had seven in seven League Cup games and a competition-winning eight in 11 UEFA Cup matches, including a hat-trick in an early round tie, and then two in the final against Wolverhampton Wanderers. He found the net twice in the first leg tie away from home, as Spurs claimed their first European title. The goal tally in the league came to 25. The prolific goal scoring continued into the 1972/73 season, with 33 goals, as the club claimed their second League Cup in three years. Chivers struck twice against Liverpool in the quarter-final, before getting a vital goal in the semi-final. The club had another good run in the UEFA Cup reaching the semi-finals, with Chivers again producing the goods with eight goals in ten matches. Another six-goal run helped Spurs to another final in the 1974 UEFA Cup including one in the semi-final win. He appeared in his final game for the club in April 1976 before moving to Swiss side Servette. He represented a few other teams before ending his playing days in the 1982/83 season with English side Barnet at the age of 38.

Accomplishments

Chivers spent eight years at Spurs, scoring 174 times in 367 matches. He was the club's leading scorer in European competitions with 22 goals at the time. He won the UEFA Cup once, and the League Cup twice with the club. For the England national team, Chivers netted 13 times in 24 matches between 1971 and 1973.

Summary: Martin Chivers is the club's fourth top goalscorer of all-time 'Big Chiv' has been described as "looking like a target man but playing like an angel" and was known for his pace and natural strength.

JERMAIN DEFOE

Born: 7th of October 1982
Debut: 2004
Nationality: English
Position: Striker
Height: 5 ft 7 in (1.71 m)
Major Trophies: 1

Early Career

Jermain Colin Defoe was born in Beckton, London to parents of Caribbean descent. He played five-a-side football and competed for the famous Sunday league side Senrab, before being invited to join the FA National School of Excellence in 1997 aged 14. After playing for Charlton Athletic's youth team, Defoe controversially decided to turn pro at rivals West Ham United in 1999. Charlton was awarded £1.4m in compensation. He made his senior debut in September 2000 and was sent on loan to Second Division side Bournemouth where he scored in a record ten successive games and 18 in 29 league games in total.

Later Career

Defoe moved across London to Tottenham Hotspur in February 2004 for £6m plus Bobby Zamora and scored again on his debut a few days later. He ended the season with seven goals in 15 games, before netting his first hat-trick ten months later against Southampton. He was voted the club's player of the year for 2004. He had a personal best stint of 48 appearances for the club in the 2006/07 season and managed his 50th goal for the team. He left for Portsmouth for £7.5m in 2008 but returned a year later for £15.75m. Defoe helped the club reach the League Cup Final with a strike in the semi-final against Burnley. In September 2009, he scored an overhead kick after only 38 seconds in a match against champions Manchester United. He then smashed in a Premier League record five goals in a 9-1 rout of Wigan Athletic in November, with his first three goals coming in the space of only seven minutes early in the second half. It was the second quickest hat-trick in the history of the Premier League. He produced his third hat-trick of the season in an FA Cup tie, to end the campaign with 24 goals. He played at the 2010 World Cup and scored the winning goal against Slovenia to ensure England's progress into the knockout stage. He scored his 100th Premier League goal towards the end of the 2010/11 season, before becoming the highest goal scorer for the club in European club competition with 23, after striking in five consecutive Europa League fixtures in 2013. He left to sign a lucrative deal with MLS side Toronto FC where he played just one season before returning to the Premier League for a successful spell at Sunderland. He then played for Bournemouth and Rangers before a brief spell back at Sunderland. He decided to retire in March 2022 at the age of 39.

Accomplishments

In two separate spells with the club, Defoe scored 143 goals in 362 matches for Spurs over eleven seasons putting him sixth on the all-time scorer's list. In his career, he produced 305 goals in 763 games. He won the League Cup with Spurs and the Scottish Premiership with Rangers. He scored at least a goal in 19 Premier League seasons and holds the record for most goals as a substitute in the league with 22. Defoe is currently the ninth-highest goalscorer in Premier League history. For the England national team, he scored 20 goals in 57 internationals and was honoured with an OBE in 2018.

Summary: Jermain Defoe is one of Tottenham's and the Premier League's great strikers averaging almost a goal every other game throughout his career. He was known as a poacher who used his excellent positioning and movement to outwit defences and score.

CHRISTIAN ERIKSEN

Born: 14th of February 1992
Debut: 2013
Nationality: Danish
Position: Midfielder
Height: 6 ft 0 in (1.82 m)
Major Trophies: 0

Early Career

Christian Dannemann Eriksen was born in the town of Middelfart in Denmark. He started playing football for the academy of the local team, just like his father who was now the coach. He joined Superliga team Odense Boldklub, and he was soon having trials at several big European clubs. In October 2008, Eriksen signed with Dutch giants Ajax for around £850k where he played with the youth squad before making his senior debut in January 2010. He helped the club to win its first league title in seven years in 2011, the first of three successive championships.

Later Career

He joined Tottenham in the infamous 2013 summer transfer window where Spurs spent £109.5m on new players, £11m of which was for the Dane. He made his debut two weeks later, before netting a fine first goal five days later in a Europa League game. He pocketed two goals as Spurs levelled against Southampton at 2-2 from 0-2 behind, before providing the assist in a 3-2 win. By the end of the season, Eriksen had scored ten goals and 13 assists and was named the club player of the season. In the 2014/15 season, he was the saviour with three late winners in three months and was at hand with two strikes as Spurs won their League Cup semi-final 3-2 on aggregate to reach the final, including a 25-yard curling free kick. He played in every Premier

League match that season. With 13 assists, Spurs managed third place in the league and qualification for the Champions League during the 2015/16 season, and with another 15 assists, Eriksen guided the side to second place the following season. Early in the 2017/18 season, he recorded his 33rd goal in the Premier League, to become the highest-scoring Danish player in the competition. In January, he struck his 50th goal for Spurs after only 11 seconds versus Manchester United, the third-fastest goal in the history of the Premier League. Another two goals helped the club to reach the FA Cup semis. In March 2019, he became the second player to achieve ten or more assists in four successive Premier League seasons. He appeared for the club in the 2019 Champions League Final and played his last game for the team in early 2020, before joining Italian side Inter Milan with six months left on his contract. In June 2021, at Euro 2020, Eriksen collapsed on the pitch playing for Denmark after suffering from cardiac arrest. There were fears he would not survive but he managed a speedy recovery. After being unable to play in Serie A due to his newly installed heart monitor, he returned to the Premier League with Brentford in 2022.

Accomplishments

Eriksen played in 305 games for Spurs in seven seasons and scored 69 goals. He was part of the side that made Spurs' first-ever Champions League Final. He competed in 47 or more games in five successive seasons with the club. He was twice named the club's Player of the Year and was voted into the 2017/18 PFA Team of the Year. His major honours so far include three Eredivisie League titles with Ajax and a Serie A title with Inter Milan. Up to 2021, Eriksen had appeared in 109 internationals for Denmark, striking 36 times.

Summary: Christian Eriksen is described as a classic 'number 10' whose main strengths are his creativity and set-piece delivery.

PAUL GASCOIGNE

Born: 27th of May 1967
Debut: 1988
Nationality: English
Position: Midfielder
Height: 5 ft 10 in (1.77 m)
Major Trophies: 1

Early Career

Paul John Gascoigne was born in Gateshead, North East England. He had a challenging childhood but was signed up by boyhood club Newcastle United as a schoolboy in 1980, after having had trials with different clubs. Four years later he became a professional and made his debut in April 1985, aged just 17. Newcastle chairman Stan Seymour Jr famously described Gascoigne as "George Best without brains". He scored his first senior goal five months later. He was named the PFA Young Player of the Year in 1988, before deciding to move south to Tottenham Hotspur later in the year for a British record signing of £2.2m, despite promising Sir Alex Ferguson he would sign for Manchester United. It was Spurs' offer of a £100,000 signing-on fee to buy his family a house that contributed to his decision.

Later Career

He helped Spurs rise from sixth to third in the league in the 1989/90 season and smashed in four goals in a League Cup game against Hartlepool in September 1990. Gascoigne had already put in some fine displays during England's run to the semi-finals of the World Cup earlier in the year. He was named as the Sports Personality of the Year, as well as the club's player of the year. He netted six goals in the FA Cup run of 1991, including a 30-yard free kick in the semi-final win over arch-rivals Arsenal at Wembley. He was injured in the final but

Spurs went on to win the game against Notts Forest. During this time, Spurs were suffering with financial problems, and there was talk of Gascoigne moving away from the club to raise funds. The cup final injury saw him miss the entire 1991/92 season. He eventually departed to join Italian side Lazio a year later for £5.5m. After three seasons in Italy, he signed for Scottish team Rangers for a club-record £4.3m in 1995. He struck a memorable goal against rivals Celtic, before bagging a hat-trick in the penultimate game of the season as the team won the title in 1996. Gascoigne produced one of the greatest goals in international football in the 1996 Euros hosted in England. Playing against old rivals Scotland at Wembley, he lifted the ball over the defender's head before volleying into the bottom corner. From Rangers, Gascoigne moved to Middlesbrough, whom he helped to promotion to the Premier League. He later moved to Everton, before playing his final game in English football in September 2004, having moved around several clubs over the years.

Accomplishments

Gascoigne played 112 times for Spurs scoring 33 goals, winning the FA Cup in 1991. He scored 39 goals in 104 games for Rangers, winning two league titles, and two domestic cups. In total, he scored 110 goals in 468 career matches. He appeared 57 times for England and scored 10 goals. He was inducted into the English Football Hall in 2002.

Summary: Paul Gascoigne was one of the most naturally talented footballers England has ever produced. Capable of acts of genius on the pitch, he suffered from personal issues off the pitch due to his addictive personality including alcohol and gambling. He has been praised by many of his peers for his ability and reputation as a prankster with Gary Lineker describing him as "the most naturally gifted technical footballer that I played with".

ALAN GILZEAN

Born: 22nd of October 1938
Debut: 1964
Nationality: Scottish
Position: Striker
Height: 6 ft 0 in (1.82 m)
Major Trophies: 5

Early Career

Alan John Gilzean was born in the city of Perth, Scotland. He played for a local junior side before signing as an amateur with professional Scottish side Dundee in 1956 aged 17. He signed as a professional a year later, before making his senior debut over two years later, after serving his National Service duty. He helped the club win its one and only Scottish Division One title in 1961/62, with 24 league goals in 29 games. The following season, he helped the club reach the semi-finals of the European Cup, scoring in the second leg tie against eventual champions AC Milan. When he left the club after seven years, he had scored a staggering 113 league goals in only 134 matches.

Later Career

Gilzean joined Spurs in December 1964 for £72,500, despite interest from other big clubs, and played his first game against Everton a week later. In an FA Cup match in 1966, he scored a memorable hat-trick to help Spurs beat Burnley 4-3 with a late goal. He was in the team when Spurs won the FA Cup for the fifth time in 1967 in front of 100, 000 spectators at Wembley Stadium. He formed an effective goal-scoring partnership alongside crowd favourite Jimmy Greaves, and together they were referred to by fans as the "G-Men". After Greaves left in 1970, Gilzean then found a new strike partner in Martin Chivers, and the pair helped Spurs to win the League Cup in

1971. He scored four goals in seven games during the competition. The following year Spurs competed in the first-ever all-English final of the UEFA Cup against Wolverhampton Wanderers and came out victors, their maiden European triumph. Gilzean scored in the quarter-final victory against UTA Arad, as well as getting a hat-trick earlier on in the tournament, giving him six goals in total. His final honour with the club was another League Cup success in 1973. Gilzean's final game for the club was the 1974 UEFA Cup Final against Feyenoord, having scored his final goal in the last game of the season. He then went on to play for a short while in South Africa, before being awarded a testimonial by Spurs in November 1974. Gilzean stated, whilst playing, that he disliked football and had no intention of furthering his career after playing but he did manage for a short while.

Accomplishments

Gilzean appeared in 439 games for Tottenham Hotspur and scored 133 goals. He was victorious in the Scottish League with Dundee once, before winning the FA Cup and UEFA Cup once as well as the League Cup twice with Spurs. He played in 22 internationals for Scotland, scoring 12 goals in eight years. He was inducted into the Scottish Football and Spurs Hall of Fame in 2009 and 2013 respectively.

Summary: Alan Gilzean enjoyed a glittering career as a Tottenham player, he changed his style of play from being the main goalscorer to being an intelligent and creative forward who would supply his strike partner. He was well known for his passing and playmaking. He earned the moniker "The King of White Hart Lane" while at Spurs. He passed away in July 2018.

DAVID GINOLA

Born: 25th of January 1967
Debut: 1997
Nationality: French
Position: Winger
Height: 6 ft 1 in (1.86 m)
Major Trophies: 1

Early Career

Born in the village of Gassin, France, David Ginola-Ceze started his club career with French side SC Toulon in 1985 and made his first professional appearance at the age of 18. He moved around a couple of other clubs, before joining Paris Saint-Germain at the age of 25 in early 1992. In the 1992/93 season, Ginola scored a goal in the Coupe de France Final and appeared in the semi-finals of the UEFA Cup.

Later Career

With 13 goals, he helped the club win its second-ever league title in the 1993/94 season, making him the side's top goalscorer for the campaign. A year later, despite being linked with Barcelona, he joined Newcastle United and was pipped to the title twice by Manchester United in his two seasons there. Spurs then signed Ginola in July 1997 for £2.5m. He made his debut a month later against Manchester United. His first league goal came towards the end of October. He ended the season with six Premier League goals, which were instrumental in helping the club avoid relegation. He was named the club's Player of the Year. He won his first and only trophy with the club in the 1999 League Cup final, having scored a memorable goal against quadruple-chasing Manchester United with a superb long-range strike in the quarter-final tie. Spurs beat Leicester City in the final. Then in the FA Cup, he netted a fine low strike against

Wimbledon, before hitting a 25-yard volley versus Leeds United. This was followed by a stunning goal against Barnsley after gliding past several players on a solo run. He ended with three goals in six FA Cup games as Spurs reached the semi-finals. By the end of the year, Ginola picked up both the Footballers' Association Player and the Football Writers' Footballer of the Year awards. He was the first player in Premiership history to win the award while at a club that finished outside of the top four. His third and final season saw him provide the most assists for the club. Ginola left Spurs in 2000 and moved to Aston Villa in August for £3m. He then played for Everton before hanging up his boots in May 2002. He took up acting after retiring and became a football pundit working for many channels. In March 2019, he came back to Spurs to play for the legends team against Inter Milan at the club's new Tottenham Hotspur Stadium.

Accomplishments

Ginola totalled 22 goals in 124 matches for Spurs including 13 in 100 league games in three seasons. A career tally saw him net over 100 goals in over 600 games. He won the League Cup once with Tottenham Hotspur and the Division 1 title with PSG. He appeared in 17 internationals for France and scored three goals. He was a Spurs Hall of Fame inductee in 2008.

Summary: David Ginola, with flair in abundance, was one of the most flamboyant players of his day, capable of producing magical moments. He was also notorious for his difficult character and lack of discipline both on and off the pitch, maybe the reason he didn't spend more than three years at a club in England. Ginola is fondly remembered by Spurs fans for his extravagant forward play and personality off the pitch.

JIMMY GREAVES

Born: 20th of February 1940
Debut: 1961
Nationality: English
Position: Striker
Height: 5 ft 8 in (1.73 m)
Major Trophies: 5

Early Career

James Peter Greaves was born in Manor Farm, Essex (now London) and was signed by Chelsea in 1955 as an apprentice. He settled in quickly with the youth team and scored 122 goals during the 1956/57 campaign. He turned professional in the summer of 1957, though spent eight weeks working at a steel company to supplement his income during the summer break. He scored on his First Division league debut in August 1957 aged just 17 against, of all teams, Spurs.

Later Career

He recorded 41 goals in 40 league games during the 1960/61 season which saw a run of three hat-tricks, four goals in a game twice, and one five-goal game. He was the youngest footballer to reach the 100-goal mark in the English league at the age of 20. In the final game of the season, also his last game for Chelsea, Greaves was made captain for the day and he responded by grabbing four goals, his 13th hat-trick for the club. A move to Italian giants AC Milan followed in 1961. After just a few games, he wanted to return to London and joined Spurs for £99,999 so that he wouldn't be burdened as the first £100,000 player. He bagged a hat-trick in his first game for the club and collected nine goals in seven games as Spurs won the 1962 FA Cup, scoring a goal three minutes into the final. He was the top scorer in the league with 37 goals in 41 games in 1962/63, including three hat-tricks and one four-goal haul. Greaves also added two more goals in the final, as Spurs became the first British team to win a European trophy, the Cup Winners' Cup. The prolific scoring continued into the 1963/64 season with 35 league goals in 41 outings. including four more hat-tricks. Greaves was in the starting line-up for England at the 1966 World Cup but did not play in the final despite being fit. He was injured in the group stage and manager Alf Ramsey kept faith in Greaves' replacement Geoff Hurst who would become the first man to score a World Cup Final hat-trick. He ended the 1968/69 year as the league's top scorer for the sixth and final time. He appeared for Spurs for the final time in January 1970. Among his records, he became the club's all-time top goalscorer, the top scorer in First Division football, and produced a club record 15 hat-tricks. He was honoured with a testimonial in October 1972. In March 1970, Greaves joined West Ham United as part exchange in Martin Peters' transfer to White Hart Lane.

Accomplishments

Greaves scored a club-record 266 goals in 379 games for Spurs. He won the FA Cup twice and the European Cup Winners' Cup once. For Chelsea, he scored 132 goals in 169 matches and he won a Serie A title with AC Milan. Greaves scored a record 357 goals in the First Division which, together with the 9 goals at A.C. Milan, meant he had scored 366 goals in the top five European leagues, a record that lasted until 2017 when it was surpassed by Cristiano Ronaldo. He appeared in 57 international matches for England and scored 44 goals. He was a member of the 1966 World Cup-winning team. He was honoured with an MBE in 2021 and was an English Football Hall of Fame inductee.

Summary: Jimmy Greaves is one of the greatest goal scorers England has ever produced. He cited his relaxed attitude as the reason for his assured composure and confidence. He passed away in 2021.

GLENN HODDLE

Born: 27th of October 1957
Debut: 1975
Nationality: English
Position: Midfielder
Height: 6 ft 0 in (1.83 m)
Major Trophies: 4

Early Career

Glenn Hoddle grew up in Essex having been born in London and was a Spurs fan growing up. He was invited to train with the club after being spotted playing in a local school cup final. He joined them as a junior player a year later at the age of 12 and made his senior debut for the team in August 1975, aged just 17. In February on his first league start, he struck a spectacular winning goal past the England goalkeeper Peter Shilton with a long-range shot against Stoke City.

Later Career

Hoddle helped Spurs to gain promotion to the First Division in 1977/78, a year after being relegated. He netted 19 goals in 41 league games during the 1979/80 season and was voted the PFA Young Player of the Year. He was one of the influential players as Spurs won their sixth FA Cup in 1981. He scored in the semi-final win against Wolves before beating Man City in the final. Spurs retained the FA Cup the following season, with Hoddle scoring both goals over the two legs in the final. His play guided the team to both the final of the League Cup and the semi-final of the European Cup Winners' Cup. He was one of the major factors in the team winning the 1984 UEFA Cup, despite missing the final due to injury problems. After winning their First Round tie 14-0, Hoddle was praised for his performance against the great Johan Cruyff's Feyenoord as Spurs won 6-2 on aggregate.

Cruyff was dismissive of Hoddle before their first match but after Hoddle's performance, Cruyff swapped shirts with Hoddle as a sign of respect. He scored his final goal at White Hart Lane in 1987 with a solo run from inside his own half against Oxford United. The surprise loss to Coventry City in the 1987 FA Cup final turned out to be Hoddle's final game in a Spurs shirt. Hoddle decided to pursue a career overseas where his style of play would be appreciated by continental managers and supporters. He was signed by Monaco who was managed by Arsène Wenger and the pair led the principality side to the 1988 league title. He returned to England after three-and-a-half seasons to become player-manager of Second Division Swindon Town who he led to promotion into the Premier League. before becoming player-manager of Chelsea in 1993. He retired from playing in 1995 at the age of 37. Hoddle was appointed England manager in 1996 and coached the team for three years including the 1998 World Cup before being dismissed a year later.

Accomplishments

Hoddle scored 110 goals in 490 appearances in 12 seasons and won the FA Cup twice, and the UEFA Cup once. He scored 27 goals in 69 matches for Monaco winning one league title. He appeared in 53 internationals for the England national team scoring eight goals. He also managed the team for 28 matches. He was a National Football Museum Hall of Fame inductee in 2007.

Summary: Glenn Hoddle was one of the most gifted footballers to play in the English game. He played for and managed both Spurs and England and is now a popular pundit and co-commentator.

PAT JENNINGS

Born: 12th of June 1945
Debut: 1964
Nationality: Northern Irish
Position: Goalkeeper
Height: 6 ft 0 in (1.83 m)
Major Trophies: 5

Early Career

Patrick Anthony Jennings was born in the city of Newry in Northern Ireland. He played for Irish team Shamrock Rovers when he was 11, before taking up Gaelic football until he was 16. He returned to football with his hometown team Newry Town in 1961. He was scouted by Third Division side Watford in 1963 and played in all the league games that season. At the same time, he played his first two international games for Northern Ireland at the age of 18. In June 1964, he attracted the attention of First Division Tottenham Hotspur and he was signed for £27,000.

Later Career

Jennings made his first team debut two months later against Sheffield United. He won his first trophy with the club, the FA Cup in 1967, playing in the final versus Chelsea. Early in the following season, he produced his one and only goal for the club, when he scored Spurs' second goal in the Charity Shield against Manchester United. He kicked the ball from his hands in his own area down the field and the ball bounced over the goalkeeper into the net. He claimed his second trophy with the club in 1971 when Spurs won the League Cup. The club also came third in the League. The following year, he was the star player as Tottenham Hotspur won their first UEFA Cup title, playing in an all-English final against

Wolverhampton Wanderers. In 12 matches he conceded just six goals and kept six consecutive clean sheets. A further League Cup success followed in 1973, the club's second in three years, with Jennings again conceding no goals in the final in front of 100,000 people at Wembley Stadium. Jennings became the first goalkeeper to be voted the PFA Player of the Year in 1976 and so far only one other goalkeeper, Peter Shilton, has won the award. Spurs believed Jennings was nearing the end of his career and allowed him to leave to join arch-rivals Arsenal where he played a further eight years helping the club to four Cup finals in three years. He became the first player in English football to appear in 1000 games in 1983 and competed in his farewell game in 1985 - against Spurs. He went back to his former club and played in one last game in 1986. In the 1986 World Cup Jennings appeared for the Northern Ireland team at the age of 41, making him the oldest to compete in the tournament at the time.

Accomplishments

Jennings played in a total of 590 games for Tottenham and 327 for Arsenal. With Spurs, he won the FA Cup once, the UEFA Cup once, and the League Cup twice. For Arsenal, he picked a further FA Cup. For Northern Ireland, he played in 119 internationals, a world record at the time, in a 22-year period. He was honoured with an OBE and inducted into the English Football Hall of Fame in 2003.

Summary: Pat Jennings was one of the best and longest-serving goalkeepers to play in England, and one of the greatest Northern Irish players of all-time.

CLIFF JONES

Born: 7th of February 1935
Debut: 1958
Nationality: Welsh
Position: Winger
Height: 5 ft 7 in (1.70 m)
Major Trophies: 5

Early Career

Clifford William Jones was born in Swansea, Wales into a footballing family. At the age of 12, he was selected as captain of the Swansea Schoolboys team. He turned pro at Swansea Town in 1952 aged 17 and joined his brother Bryn, who was also playing for the club. Jones made his first team debut against Bury in October 1952 and netted his maiden goal against Leeds United two games later. Having made his international debut for the Wales national team in 1954, Jones struck the winning goal in the 2-1 win versus England a year later, in just his second match for the side.

Later Career

He spent six years with Swansea scoring 47 league goals in 168 matches for the Welsh side. He joined First Division side Tottenham Hotspur in February 1958 for a record fee of £35,000. Jones made his debut against fellow London rivals Arsenal a few days later, in an entertaining 4-4 draw. In the same month, he helped Wales qualify for the finals of the World Cup tournament for the first time. He played in all five games as Wales reached the quarter-final, before losing to Brazil by just one goal scored by Pele; his first-ever goal in the competition. He managed 25 goals during the 1959/60 season and was a crucial member of the Spurs team that won a memorable double in the 1960/61 season scoring 19 goals. He mainly played right

-wing until the double-winning season but switched to left-wing in the subsequent seasons. In 1962, Spurs turned down a world-record £125,000 fee from Italian giants Juventus. He stayed and became a vital provider for the likes of Bobby Smith and Jimmy Greaves. Further success followed in the 1962 FA Cup, scoring four goals on the way to the final, including one each in the quarter-final and semi-final wins. Spurs became the first British team to win a major European trophy when they triumphed in the 1963 European Cup Winners' Cup. Jones again contributed with a goal in the quarter-final and a goal in the semi-final. He scored on his final appearance for the club against Manchester United in October 1968. He moved to Fulham for two seasons and played for a few other teams before retiring in 1971 aged 36.

Accomplishments

Jones played in 378 matches for Spurs and scored 159 goals in 10 seasons. He won one First Division title, one Cup Winners' Cup, and three FA Cups. For the Wales national team, he earned 59 caps and netted 16 goals. He was inducted into the National Football Museum Hall of Fame and received an honorary fellowship from the University of Wales.

Summary: Cliff Jones was a pivotal member of the Spurs team in the late '50s and early '60s in one of the club's great sides. He was noted for his pace and considered one of the best wingers in the world at the time. Jones is fifth on Spurs' all-time goalscoring charts and the record scorer who wasn't a striker.

ROBBIE KEANE

Born: 8th of July 1980
Debut: 2002
Nationality: Irish
Position: Forward
Height: 5 ft 9 in (1.75 m)
Major Trophies: 1

Early Career

Robert David Keane was born in the Tallaght area of Dublin, Ireland. He started playing football for local club side Fettercairn and also played Gaelic football until he was 15. He was signed by second tier side Wolverhampton Wanderers just before his 16th birthday in 1996 and played for the youth team. He made his first-team debut a year later in August 1997, aged 17, scoring two goals on his debut. Keane was the club's top goalscorer with 16 goals during the 1998/99 season.

Later Career

After two seasons at Molineux, he was transferred to Premier League side Coventry City in 1999 for £6m, to become the most expensive British teenager. He again scored two goals on his first team debut and scored 12 goals in his first Premier League season. He then moved abroad to Italian giants Inter Milan in 2000 but failed to settle and he was loaned to Leeds United, after just 6 appearances. Leeds signed him permanently the next season but again he was on the move after just one season when he signed for Spurs in 2002 for £7m. He won a penalty for the team on his debut and finished the season with 13 goals, the club's top scorer, including a spectacular hat-trick against Everton. In the 2005/06 season, he was again the leading goalscorer for the club with 16 goals and was given the captaincy on a few occasions. Keane had a personal best tally to date of 22 goals in the 2006/07 season, with

15 of his goals coming in his final 15 games. The season also saw him play his 200th game for the club which was followed by him joining a select group of players with 100 Premier League goals. 2007 saw Keane record 19 league goals, the best in the Premier League for the calendar year, and a superb 31 goals and 13 assists in 40 matches from January to December. He won the first major trophy of his career when Spurs triumphed in the 2008 League Cup, and by collecting another 15 goals during the season, he became the first player from the club to score ten or more goals in six successive Premier League seasons. He then moved to boyhood club Liverpool in 2008 for £19m but returned to Spurs after just seven months at Anfield. Upon his return, he was appointed vice-captain and often skippered the side due to Ledley King's injury problems. He scored four goals in a game against Burnley in 2009, before being loaned to Celtic and West Ham United. He then enjoyed a successful 6-year spell with MLS side LA Galaxy where he scored 104 goals in 165 games. He had a loan spell at Aston Villa and played for Indian side ATK before retiring in 2018 aged 38.

Accomplishments

Keane appeared in 306 matches for Spurs scoring 122 goals. He scored 325 career goals in 737 appearances for 11 clubs. He won the League Cup once with Spurs and three MLS Cups with the LA Galaxy. For his national team, the Republic of Ireland, he played in a record-breaking 146 games and scored a national-record 68 goals. He is the only international player in history to have scored at least a goal in 19 consecutive years and was the team captain for ten years.

Summary: Robbie Keane is one of the most celebrated footballers in Ireland's history and is known for his goal celebration where he performed a cartwheel followed by a forward roll.

LEDLEY KING

Born: 12th of October 1980
Debut: 1999
Nationality: English
Position: Defender
Height: 6 ft 2 in (1.88 m)
Major Trophies: 1

Early Career

Ledley Brenton King was born in the Bow area of London. In his youth, he played for Senrab FC, a Sunday league side famous for producing many professional players. He joined the Spurs academy in July 1996 as a trainee and made his first-team debut against Liverpool in May 1999, becoming a regular for the team over a year later. He initially played in midfield under George Graham but eventually settled in central defence. His first goal came in December 2000 after only ten seconds against Bradford City, the quickest ever goal in the Premier League at the time and a record that lasted for over 18 years. He made his England debut in 2002.

Later Career

King was made the club captain in 2005. In 2006, he led the side to a 2-1 victory over Chelsea – the club's first league win over them in 16 years. King suffered from injury problems throughout 2006 and for the next couple of years but managed to skipper the side to another 2-1 win over Chelsea, this time in the 2008 League Cup Final to pick up the first trophy of his career. He competed in only four league games in 2007/08. The injury problems continued to plague King throughout the 2008/09 campaign. He managed his 200th league appearance for the club, and then captained Spurs again in the League Cup Final of 2009, keeping a clean sheet for 120 minutes, before the team lost on penalties. The consistent knee problems meant King was unable to train with the team and did mostly his own gym exercises to keep fit. With no immediate cure or treatment for his injuries, King was praised for being able to compete in the top tier of English football at a high level. In May 2010, King helped Spurs to their highest ever finish in the Premier League of fourth position after he skippered the side to a 1-0 win away at Manchester City which secured Champions League qualification for the first time. He had a steel statue erected in his honour in a London park a year later. In July 2012, King announced his retirement from football and eventually became an ambassador for the club. He had played in 14 seasons for the team and received only eight yellow cards in his career. He was honoured with a testimonial match in May 2014 and scored the opening goal with a penalty.

Accomplishments

A true one-club man, King appeared 323 times for the club scoring 14 goals. He won the League Cup once with his one and only club. He represented England in 21 internationals including games at Euro 2004 and the 2010 World Cup, netting two goals.

Summary: Many fans and fellow professionals believe that King would have gone on to become one of the best centre backs to have played the game if not for his injuries. Thierry Henry stated he was the best defender he had played against and the only one to tackle him without resorting to fouling. He was highly commended for competing in the Premier League despite his major knee problems. He has taken up a variety of positions at the club since retiring.

JÜRGEN KLINSMANN

Born: 30th of July 1964
Debut: 1994
Nationality: German
Position: Striker
Height: 5 ft 11 in (1.81 m)
Major Trophies: 0

Early Career

Jürgen Klinsmann was born in the town of Goppingen, in West Germany. He began playing football at the age of eight for an amateur club in his hometown where he once struck 16 goals in one match. His family moved to Stuttgart and he signed up with one of the city's main football teams, Stuttgarter Kickers. He made his professional debut in 1982 playing in the Second Division, before deciding to move to nearby Bundesliga side VfB Stuttgart in 1984. He was the joint top scorer for the club in his first season there. He increased this to 19 goals in the 1987/88 season to be the league's top scorer. His biggest achievement came in 1990 when he won the World Cup with West Germany, scoring three goals during the tournament.

Later Career

Klinsmann had further stints with Inter Milan and AS Monaco, before joining Spurs in July 1994 for £2m. He arrived in England with a reputation as a diver and after scoring a header on his Spurs debut against Sheffield Wednesday, he celebrated by theatrically diving on the ground. He also struck twice in his second game against Everton. Klinsmann scored in five of his first six league games for the club and had recorded seven goals at that stage. He went on another scoring spree towards the end of the season with goals in six out of eight games, including three matches in succession. He produced 20 goals in the league and ended his maiden season with 29 goals for the club. He scored five goals in six FA Cup games, and also a hat-trick in the League Cup. He scored a late winner at Anfield to fire Spurs into the FA Cup semi-finals which he again scored in but ultimately ended in defeat to Everton. He was named the Football Writers' Footballer of the Year. Klinsmann however moved back to Germany to join Bundesliga side Bayern Munich for the following season. He was the club's top goalscorer in both his two seasons there, including a superb 15 goals in 12 games as Bayern won the UEFA Cup in 1996, with six goals in the two-leg victory over Benfica, and one in the final. Having represented West Germany for the first time in 1987, Klinsmann took part in his 100th international for Germany in September 1997 and slotted two goals past Armenia. After moving back to Spurs for the 1997/98 season, he smashed four goals past Wimbledon, before playing in his final game for the club a week later. He then became a manager, leading Germany at their home 2006 World Cup and the USA at the 2014 edition in Brazil.

Accomplishments

Klinsmann netted a total of 38 goals in 68 games in his two spells at Spurs. The league count was 29 strikes in 56 matches. In his career, he scored 284 goals in 620 games. He won the UEFA Cup with Inter Milan and Bayern Munich and a Bundesliga title with the latter. He netted 47 goals in 108 matches for Germany and is their fourth top scorer of all time. He was victorious in the World Cup once and the European Championships hosted in England in 1996.

Summary: Jürgen Klinsmann was one of Germany's greatest ever strikers and one of their most well-known footballers. A combination of his athletic achievements and his combative playing style together with his jovial personality, Klinsmann quickly became extremely popular in England; over 150,000 of his shirts were sold and now holds legendary status at Spurs despite his short time with the club.

GARY LINEKER

Born: 30th of November 1960
Debut: 1989
Nationality: English
Position: Striker
Height: 5 ft 10 in (1.77 m)
Major Trophies: 2

Early Career

Gary Winston Lineker was born in the city of Leicester, East Midlands and joined the Leicester City academy in 1976 after leaving school. He was given his middle name in honour of Winston Churchill, with whom he shares a birthday. He had also excelled at cricket whilst at school. He turned professional in 1978 and made his first team debut on New Year's Day 1979 and helped Leicester win the Second Division title. They were unable to stay up but Lineker scored 43 goals in two seasons as the club bounced back at the second time of asking. He was the top division's second-highest goalscorer during the 1983/84 season with 22 goals, before taking the joint top accolade a year later with 24 strikes. His impressive goal scoring attracted league champions Everton in 1985 who signed him in 1985 for £800,000.

Later Career

His debut came against former club Leicester and he would go on to bang in 30 goals in 41 league games, including three hat-tricks that season. He won the World Cup Golden Boot that summer with 6 goals including one in the infamous quarter-final defeat to Argentina. He was subsequently snapped up by Spanish giants Barcelona after just one season with Everton, scoring two goals on his debut. He became the highest scoring British player in the Spanish league after three seasons, before moving again, this time back to England to sign for Tottenham Hotspur in the summer of 1989 for just over £1m. He made an immediate impact with 24 league goals in his debut season as Spurs came third in the table and was again the top scorer in the league. His first trophy success, and his first major one in England, came in the 1991 FA Cup. Lineker scored two goals in the semi-final win over Arsenal, before helping Spurs defeat Nottingham Forest in the final, despite having a goal disallowed and a penalty saved. Another 28 goals in 35 league games followed in 1991/92, before he played his last game in Spurs in May 1992, scoring his final goal on the last day of the season against Manchester United. He joined Japanese side Nagoya Grampus for £2m where he played for two seasons before retiring aged 32. Lineker became a television personality after retiring, appearing in football programmes, and commercials.

Accomplishments

Lineker netted 80 goals in 138 games for Spurs across three seasons. For Barcelona, he scored 52 in 137 games, and 103 in 216 games with Leicester City. In his career, he netted 281 goals in 567 matches. His major honours included the FA Cup with Spurs and the European Cup Winners' Cup with Barcelona. In 80 international matches for England, Lineker scored 48 times making him the leading all-time scorer at the time and is still currently third on the list. He was awarded an OBE in 1992 and was an English Football Hall of Fame inductee in 2003.

Summary: Gary Lineker was one of English football's best strikers of his generation. He is known for hosting football programmes including Match of the Day as well as FA Cup Finals and England matches.

GARY MABBUTT

Born: 23rd of August 1961
Debut: 1982
Nationality: English
Position: Defender
Height: 5 ft 10 in (1.78 m)
Major Trophies: 4

Early Career

Gary Vincent Mabbutt was born in the city of Bristol and began his career with hometown club Bristol Rovers in 1979. He played over 130 league games in three years for the club, before joining First Division team Tottenham Hotspur for £105,000 in August 1982 at the age of 20 on the recommendation of club legend Bill Nicholson. He made his debut at Wembley Stadium against Liverpool in a Charity Shield game. Mabbutt scored on his league debut versus Luton Town. He saw the side win the North London derby 5-0 in April, before a 2-0 result against Manchester United and a 4-1 win over Stoke City enabled Spurs to secure a UEFA Cup spot on the last day of the season, with a fourth-place finish.

Later Career

He was noted for his excellent defensive display in the captain's absence as the team won the 1984 UEFA Cup on penalties. In the 1986/87 season, Mabbutt helped Spurs to third in the league, the semi-finals of the League Cup, and the final of the FA Cup. He had scored the team's second goal in the FA Cup Final but then scored an own goal in extra time to give Coventry victory. He appeared in 51 matches during the season. He was named the captain during the 1987/88 season, and he skippered the side to victory in the 1991 FA Cup final with a 2-1 victory over Nottingham Forest in extra time. He lifted the trophy after receiving it from Princess Diana. Mabbutt made his 500th appearance for the club in October 1993 but then sustained a fractured skull and eye socket a month later after being elbowed by Wimbledon striker John Fashanu. On his return three months later, he became the first player to wear a protective mask on the pitch. He was then unfortunate to break his leg on the opening day of the 1996/97 season, and he missed the rest of the campaign. He returned for the 1997/98 season, still as captain and played his final game for the club against Southampton in May 1998, on the last day of the season. He came on as a substitute and was given the captain's armband one final time in a game that was also Jürgen Klinsmann's last for the club. He finished as the club's second long-serving player in terms of appearances. After retiring, he became the club's ambassador and was also involved in ambassadorial work for two charities. He was invited to manage the Spurs Legends team against Inter Milan in 2019 in celebration of the new Tottenham Hotspur stadium.

Accomplishments

Mabbutt made 619 appearances for Tottenham, with 477 games in the league and 27 goals. He won the FA Cup once and the UEFA Cup once. He won 16 caps for England, recording one goal. He was honoured with an MBE in 1994, and he was also the recipient of honorary degrees in science, health, and law. His longevity is particularly impressive as he battled throughout his career against the effects of diabetes as well as two serious injuries.

Summary: Gary Mabbutt's Spurs career lasted for 16 seasons from 1982 to 1998 which included 11 as captain. He played over 750 games in his career and is second on Spurs' all-time appearance list.

DAVE MACKAY

Born: 14th of November 1934
Debut: 1959
Nationality: Scottish
Position: Midfielder/Defender
Height: 5 ft 8 in (1.73 m)
Major Trophies: 8

Early Career

David Craig Mackay was born in Edinburgh, Scotland. He was selected for the Scottish schoolboys as a teenager and then signed professional terms with Heart of Midlothian in 1952, the team he supported as a boy. He made his first team debut in November 1953 and he won his first trophy with the club in 1954, the Scottish League Cup. It was the team's first trophy in 48 years.

Later Career

Mackay then helped Hearts to triumph in the 1956 Scottish Cup, defeating Celtic 3-1 in the final. He made his international debut for Scotland in May 1957 against Spain and then captained Hearts to the Division One league championship in 1957/58, with a domestic record 132 goals. Mackay netted 12 league goals during the campaign. At the 1958 World Cup, Mackay appeared in one game for Scotland, before captaining the side for the first time four months later in just his third international. Mackay then moved to Tottenham Hotspur for £32,000 in March 1959 and made his debut a few days later against Manchester City. He started to blend well with skipper Danny Blanchflower, and the club achieved the unique League and Cup double during the 1960/61 season. In December, he scored a goal in the 36th minute as Spurs went 4-0 up against defending league champions Burnley before the match ended up in a remarkable 4-4 draw. The club defended the FA Cup in 1962 before Mackay contributed to Spurs reaching the final of the 1963 Cup Winners' Cup, with the opening goal in the second leg of the semi-final against OFK Beograd but missed the final due to injury. He was badly injured in a European tie the following season against Manchester United, and he missed almost a year and a half of football. When he returned to the team for the 1965/66 season, he was made the club captain and he skippered the side to an FA Cup success in 1967, beating Chelsea in the final. At the age of 33, Brian Clough signed him for Derby County in 1968 and he helped the side to gain promotion to the First Division. He played the final game of his career in 1972, before going on to manage a variety of teams after retiring.

Accomplishments

Mackay played in a total of 318 games for Spurs and scored 51 goals. He also made 120+ league appearances for Hearts and Derby. He won a Division One championship with Hearts, one First Division, one Cup Winners' Cup, and three FA Cups with Spurs. As manager, he won the First Division title with Derby County. For Scotland, he won 22 caps and scored four goals. He was an inaugural inductee of both the English and Scottish Football Halls of Fame.

Summary: Dave Mackay was described, by Tottenham Hotspur, as one of their greatest players and was known as 'the heartbeat' of their most successful ever team.

LUKA MODRIĆ

Born: 9th September 1985
Debut: 2008
Nationality: Croatian
Position: Midfielder
Height: 5 ft 8 in (1.72 m)
Major Trophies: 0

Early Career

Born in the city of Zadar, in the former Yugoslavia (now Croatia), Luka Modrić lived as a refugee during the war in his country. He began playing football whenever he could and eventually joined NK Zadar as a youth. He signed his first professional contract with Dinamo Zagreb in the 2005/06 season and helped the team win three consecutive league titles. After being courted by many teams, it was Spurs who won his signature in 2008 for a joint club-record fee. of £16.5m. He selected the number 14 number in honour of Johan Cruyff. He had a tough start to his career and critics including Arséne Wenger suggested he was too slight to play in the Premier League.

Later Career

Modrić scored his first goal four months later in a UEFA Cup game, and his first league goal came three days later. He impressed with his playmaking, as Spurs finished fourth in the league in 2009/10, and reached the semi-finals of the FA Cup. The club repeated the feat in the 2011/12 campaign. He played in over 40 games per season in three of the four years he was at the club. He also helped Spurs reach the quarter-finals of the Champions League in 2011, assisting in a goal in the win over Inter Milan, before scoring against Werder Bremen. He ended the season with a club-best 62.5 passes per match, with an 87% pass accuracy during the league campaign. He netted with two

25-yard efforts during the 2011/12 season including one against Liverpool. Chelsea relentlessly pursued his signature and made a final offer of £40m however it was Real Madrid who signed him in August 2012 for around £30m. At the end of his first year, he was voted the worst signing of the season by Spanish newspaper Marca. Just two years later, however, he received the LFP award for the "Best Midfielder" in La Liga. That season he was part of Real Madrid's 'La Decima' side who won their first Champions League title in 12 years. He assisted the first goal as Real beat Bayern Munich in the semi-finals in his 100th game for the club and then provided the corner as for Sergio Ramos' stoppage time equaliser in the final before winning in extra time. Real won the competition three years in succession before Modric was honoured with the 'Golden Ball' at the 2018 World Cup competition for being the best player of the tournament. He led his team Croatia to their first-ever World Cup Final. He won both the Ballon d'Or and the UEFA Men's Player of the Year award. In October 2021, he captained Real for the first time, before competing in his 100th Champions League match just over a month later.

Accomplishments

Modrić made 159 appearances for Spurs, scoring 17 goals in four seasons. For Real Madrid, he has so far scored over 30 goals in 430+ appearances. He has won the La Liga three times, and the Champions League five times with Real Madrid. He has played for Croatia in a record 148 internationals and recorded 21 goals as of 2022.

Summary: Luka Modrić is one of the best midfielders of his generation and most technically gifted players to ever wear the Spurs shirt.

BILL NICHOLSON

Born: 26th of January 1919
Debut: 1938
Nationality: English
Position: Midfielder
Height: 5 ft 9 in (1.75 m)
Major Trophies (Player): 3
Major Trophies: (Manager): 12

Early Career

Born in the seaside town of Scarborough, in Yorkshire, England, William Edward Nicholson was invited by Tottenham Hotspur to have a trial with them at the age of 17 after leaving school. He became part of the ground staff and played with the team's nursery club. He turned professional in August 1938, and his first league game followed two months later. During the Second World War, Nicholson played in a few matches and became a PE instructor training new recruits.

Later Career

In 1946, he went back to Spurs and helped the team to win the League championship in 1950/51. He initially played at centre half for two seasons after the war, then moved to right half for a further six years. He played in his first international match for England in May 1951 and netted a goal against Portugal with his first touch after only 19 seconds. This was his one and only game for his country. He appeared for the final time for Spurs in 1955 and enrolled on a coaching course run by the Football Association. He became part of the coaching staff at the club after his playing days were over and was promoted to coach of the first team a year later. Nicholson was also assistant manager for England during the 1958 World Cup. In October, he was named the new manager of Spurs, with the club sixth from bottom in the league. In his first game in charge, Spurs recorded a then club record 10-4 win over Everton at home. Two seasons later, Nicholson led Spurs to the English domestic double, winning both the League title, with 115 goals, and the FA Cup. This was followed by another FA Cup the following season, as well as a run to the semi-finals of the European Cup where they were defeated by Benfica. However, Nicholson helped put that right in 1963, when he managed the team to a Cup Winners' Cup triumph, becoming the first British side to win a major European competition. A third FA Cup success in seven years was achieved in 1967 when they beat Chelsea in the first-ever all-London FA Cup Final. Nicholson's inspired leadership guided Spurs to another three major trophies in the space of three seasons. As the 1970s wore on, Nicholson became increasingly disillusioned with football, in particular, the increased player wages and the endemic hooliganism leading to his resignation early in the 1974/75 season. He worked as a club consultant a couple of years later and was then named as club president in 1991.

Accomplishments

Nicholson played 314 league matches for Spurs, scoring six times, winning the Second Division in 1950 and incredibly, the First Division a season later. As manager, he won the First Division once including Spurs' last, the FA Cup three times, the UEFA Cup once, the Cup Winners' Cup once, and the League Cup twice in a 16-year career. For England, he attained one cap and scored one goal. He was awarded an OBE in 1975 and inducted into the English Football Hall of Fame in 2003. He was honoured with a testimonial in 2001.

Summary: Bill Nicholson remains Tottenham's greatest ever manager and was a true one-club man having spent an amazing 55 years at the club. He passed away in October 2004 but he will never be forgotten.

STEVE PERRYMAN

Born: 21st of December 1951
Debut: 1969
Nationality: English
Position: Defender/Midfielder
Height: 5 ft 9 in (1.76 m)
Major Trophies: 7

Early Career

Born in the Ealing area of London, Stephen John Perryman appeared in friendly matches for his school team before being given the opportunity to play in competitive district and schools games. He played for the England Schoolboys before signing for Spurs in 1967 as a youth team and reserve team player. Perryman made his first team debut in September 1969. He won the 1970 FA Youth Cup alongside Scotsman Graeme Souness. He soon became a regular in the team and impressed with his work in midfield. At the age of 20, he captained the Spurs team for the first time in 1971 and was appointed full-time to the post four years later.

Later Career

His first success with the club came in the League Cup in 1971, with a 2-0 victory over Aston Villa, including a vital clearance off the goal-line. He struck two long-range shots past AC Milan in 1972, as Spurs reached the final of the inaugural UEFA Cup and went on to triumph in the final. Another League Cup honour followed in 1973, and the team also reached the final of the UEFA Cup in 1974. He was appointed club captain in 1975, however, the club were relegated to the Second Division at the end of the 1976/77 season. Perryman helped lead the side back to the top flight after one season. With the signing of

Argentinians Ossie Ardiles and Ricky Villa, the club got back to winning ways with successive victories in the 1981 and 1982 FA Cup Finals. He followed in the footsteps of Joe Harvey and Danny Blanchflower by skippering Tottenham to successive FA Cup wins. Perryman played in a club record 453rd league game in 1981, and his 500th career match came a year later. He played in the semi-final of the European Cup Winners' Cup in 1982, and the first leg of the 1984 UEFA Cup Final but missed the second leg as Spurs won the title on penalties. He represented Spurs for the final time in March 1986, to end with a club record 854 games over 17 years; the club's longest-serving footballer. He had scored at least one goal in each season. He joined Oxford United, and then went to London side Brentford as player-manager. His last game came in 1990. He went back to Spurs to become their assistant manager in 1994 and became director of football at Exeter City in 2003 until his temporary retirement in March 2018.

Accomplishments

Perryman appeared in 655 league games for Tottenham Hotspur in 17 seasons and netted 31 goals. He played in 854 games for the club, including 69 in the FA Cup, and 64 times in Europe; all club records. He played in over 900 games in his career. He was victorious in two FA Cups, two UEFA Cups, and two League Cups with Spurs. Perryman was also voted the Football Writers' Association Footballer of the Year in 1982 and was honoured with an MBE in 1986. He also won a league and cup in Japan as manager of Shimizu S-Pulse in 1999 and 2000.

Summary: Steve Perryman was one of the longest-serving players for Tottenham Hotspur, and also the most successful for the club with six major trophies. No man has represented the club as much as him.

TEDDY SHERINGHAM

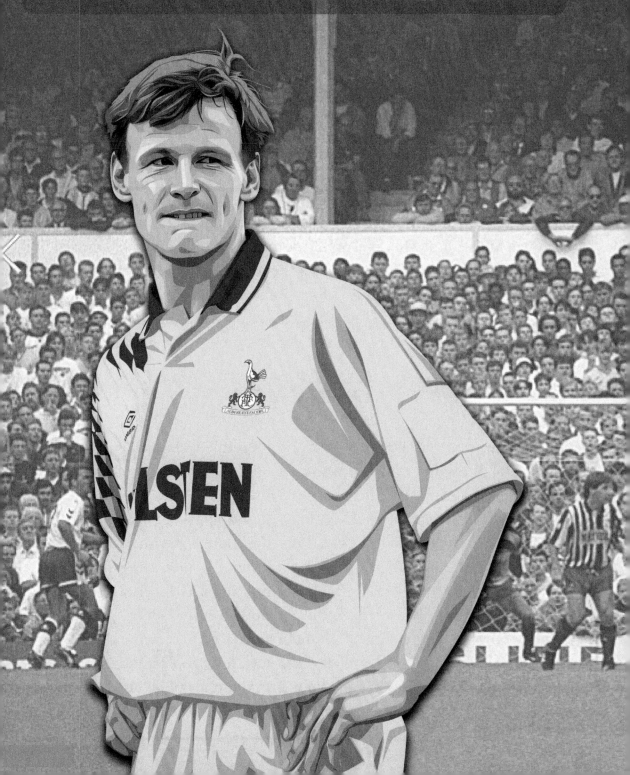

Born: 2nd of April 1966
Debut: 1992
Nationality: English
Position: Striker
Height: 6 ft 1 in (1.85 m)
Major Trophies: 0

Early Career

Edward Paul Sheringham was born in Highams Park, London. He began his youth career in 1982 with a non-league club and in a game against Millwall at the age of 16, he impressed enough to join their youth team. He scored a goal in his second professional appearance in early 1984 and was the club's top goalscorer for four seasons. After eight seasons at Millwall, he was signed by Nottingham Forest in July 1991 for £2m. He left Millwall as their all-time leading scorer.

Later Career

Sheringham netted Forest's first ever Premier League goal against Liverpool in August 1992 but was then sold a week later to Tottenham Hotspur for £2.1m. His first game for Spurs came two days later, and his first goal three days after that. In the space of five games, he netted nine times, including a hat-trick. Sheringham was the top goalscorer in the inaugural season of the Premier League with 22 goals, and he netted 28 goals in all competitions. The following season, he appeared in only 19 league games due to injury but was still the club's top goal-getter with 13. He helped the team to reach the FA Cup semi-finals during the 1994/95 season with four goals and contributed with another 23 goals. He was named as the club's Player of the Year. He was the club's top scorer again the following season with 16 league goals, and 24 in total. In June 1997 he joined Manchester United for £3.5m. He was one of the heroes when United triumphed in the Champions League Final in 1999, coming on as a substitute and striking in an injury time equaliser before providing for the winning goal moments later in one of the greatest comebacks in football. Four days earlier, he had also scored as a sub in the FA Cup Final, as the team achieved an unprecedented treble that season. Sheringham's first three trophies of his career came after 15 years as a professional. He was then given a free transfer back to Tottenham Hotspur in May 2001 where he spent two seasons. He helped Spurs to a ninth-place finish, their highest in six years, and the League Cup Final where he was denied a penalty in the dying minutes after being fouled. He hit double figures in the league in both seasons of his return. Sheringham later played for Portsmouth and West Ham as he became the oldest player to score a hat-trick in the Premier League at 37, as well as the oldest to score a goal and appear as an outfielder in the league at 40 years of age. He retired at the age of 42 in 2008 after a season at Colchester United.

Accomplishments

For Tottenham Hotspur, Sheringham appeared in 277 games and scored 124 goals. In his 25-year career, he scored over 350 goals in 926 matches. He won the Premier League three times, the Champions League once, and the FA Cup once, all with Manchester United. He played in 51 internationals for England netting 11 goals including two against The Netherlands at Euro '96. He was awarded an MBE in 2012 and was an English football Hall of Fame inductee in 2009.

Summary: Teddy Sheringham was one of the best strikers of his generation. A versatile forward, Sheringham was capable of playing as a striker and also as a supporting forward. He is currently the eleventh-highest scorer in Premier League history with 146 goals.

BOBBY SMITH

Born: 22nd of February 1933
Debut: 1955
Nationality: English
Position: Forward
Height: 5 ft 9 in (1.75 m)
Major Trophies: 6

Early Career

Robert Alfred Smith was born in the Yorkshire village of Lingdale. Whilst playing for the Redcar Boys club, he was spotted by First Division Chelsea and he signed as a schoolboy in 1947. He turned professional in 1950. Smith was part of the Chelsea side that won the First Division title in 1954/55. He wasn't a regular starter in his time at Chelsea and in December 1955, he moved across London to join Spurs for £18,000. He helped the club survive relegation after joining when the club were second from bottom in the league.

Later Career

During the 1957/58 season, Smith was the top goalscorer in the league with 36 goals as Spurs came third in the table. He equalled the club record for the most individual goals in a season and netted two unique hat-tricks against both the Manchester clubs, United and City. The former treble was his first hat-trick for the club and came in an amazing 4-3 win away from home. Having scored a fine goal against them earlier in the season, Smith then put two past Arsenal in a manic 4-4 draw, before racking up his third hat-trick of the campaign soon after. Another four goals were put past Aston Villa, as the club recorded 93 goals during the season. With 32 goals, he was the joint top goalscorer in the 1958/59 season First Division alongside strike partner Jimmy Greaves. He netted two against Manchester United in a 2-2 draw, four versus Everton in a record 10-4 win, and then another quadruple in an end of season game against West Bromwich Albion. He had recorded a total of 85 goals in two seasons in all competitions for the club. Another 25 goals in the First Division followed in 1959/60, before being part of the team that won the famous double in the 1960/61 season. With Bill Nicholson as manager, Smith produced 33 goals in 43 matches in both the league and cup competitions. He netted the first goal in the FA Cup Final, before helping towards the second as Spurs defeated Leicester City 2-0. He had been suffering from recurring injuries but managed to score again in the 1962 FA Cup Final victory. His final trophy with the club was the the 1963 Cup Winners' Cup. Smith finished his career with Spurs as the club's leading all-time goal scorer, including 12 hat-tricks. He had been top scorer for the club in six successive seasons. He moved to Brighton & Hove Albion in 1964 and helped the team to win the Fourth Division title in 1965. He retired in May 1969 after a short spell at Hastings United.

Accomplishments

Smith racked up a then club-record 208 goals in 317 games for Spurs, including 176 in 271 league games. He won the First Division title once, the FA Cup twice, and the Cup Winners' Cup once with Spurs. He was capped 15 times by the England national team and scored an impressive 13 goals which included two goals in the 9–3 defeat of Scotland at Wembley in 1961.

Summary: Bobby Smith was one of the toughest and hardest players to play for Spurs and was noted for his strength and aerial ability despite his relatively small frame. He passed away in September 2010.

RICKY VILLA

Born: 18th of August 1952

Debut: 1978

Nationality: Argentinian

Position: Midfielder

Height: 6 ft 1 in (1.85 m)

Major Trophies: 2

Early Career

Ricardo Julio Villa was born in the town of Roque Perez, Buenos Aires, in Argentina. It was down on the family farm that Villa spent all his spare time playing football, dribbling around machinery and livestock and pretending he was the next Alfredo di Stefano. He began playing for the local side Quilmes in 1970 at the age of 17. After making over 100 appearances for them, he then moved on to Atletico de Tucuman, before heading to top Argentinian side Racing Club in 1976 for a record transfer fee. Villa was selected for the Argentina World Cup squad in 1978, and he made two appearances as a substitute, as his country went on to win the tournament.

Later Career

After the success, Villa made a surprise move to England in July 1978, alongside his World Cup teammate Ossie Ardiles. They were welcomed with a ticker tape parade, and Villa celebrated by scoring on his debut for the club against Nottingham Forest a month later. His greatest moment with Spurs came in the 1981 FA Cup final. Having scored in the semi-final replay win, he then appeared in the Centenary/100th final of the competition in May. The match was drawn 1-1 against Manchester City, and the replay took place five days later. Villa was substituted midway through the second half in the first leg but was back in the starting line-up for the second match. He made an immediate impression by scoring the first goal in the eighth minute to give Spurs the early lead. City went 2-1 up before Spurs equalised with 20 minutes to go. Six minutes later, Villa was given the ball from the left wing around 30 yards from goal. He then went on a solo run past multiple City defenders before entering the penalty area and striking a right foot shot past the advancing goalkeeper to give Spurs a 3-2 lead. It turned out to be the winning goal. The Spurs squad were invited to meet Princess Anne after the final where Villa and Ardiles infamously turned up in jeans. In 2001, his goal was voted the Wembley goal of the century. He fired in a memorable hat-trick against Wolverhampton Wanderers as the new West Stand was unveiled at White Hart Lane in February 1982. He missed the 1982 FA Cup Final due to the Falklands conflict between his country and the UK. Villa was at the ground to watch the first match, as Spurs again won the title after a replay. He played his last game for the club in 1983. He later played in the USA and Colombia, before going back to Argentina. He got involved in politics during the '90s and became a coach.

Accomplishments

Villa made 179 appearances for the team and netted 25 goals winning the FA Cup once. He won 17 caps for Argentina, scoring one goal. He won the World Cup once but his appearances were limited after that due to the emergence of a young Diego Maradona. He was a Tottenham Hotspur Hall of Fame inductee in 2008.

Summary: Ricky Villa was a tall midfield player with a powerful build. He is best remembered for his goal in the 1981 FA Cup Final.

You have now come to the end of the book, I really hope you have enjoyed it and have learnt lots of awesome facts about these Tottenham Hotspur legends to impress your mates and family.

As a small independent publisher, positive reviews left on our books go a long way to attracting new readers who share your passion for the game.

If you are able to take a few minutes out of your day to leave a review it would be greatly appreciated!

If you spot any issues you would like to raise, please do **email me before leaving a negative review** with any comments you may have.

I will be more than happy to liaise with you and can offer refunds or updated copies if you are unhappy with your purchase.

kieran.brown2402@gmail.com